MW01296949

Christians In Recovery®
Workbook & Meeting Guide

by

S. O. Brennan
Executive Director, Christians in Recovery®

CIR Workbook & Meeting Guide

Published by Christians-in-Recovery® Inc.

Second Printing
Christians in Recovery® Inc. is a 501(c)(3) non-profit corporation. It is governed by a Board of Directors that meets on a regular basis and is supported by people like you who become members and/or donate. This book is also available as software for use with your computer. To order go to:

http://Self-HelpSoftware.com/Workbook

To order additional copies of this book go to:

http://Christians-in-Recovery.org/Workbook

Cover design by Christine Cartwright
www.DigitellDesign.com

ISBN: 1453758526
EAN-13: 9781453758526

http://Christians-In-Recovery.org

Printed in the United States of America

Dedicated to: All of the members, volunteers and donors who make
Christians in Recovery possible.

CIR is supported by those who join as members, volunteer and donate. Please visit our web site to learn more about:

Joining:
https://christians-in-recovery.org/Join

Benefits of Membership:
http://christians-in-recovery.org/Membership_Benefits

Donating:
https://christians-in-recovery.org/Give

Acknowledgment:
Many thanks and blessings to
Dr. Clara Thore
for her many hours of editing, expertise and support.

Table of Contents

Part II: Working the Steps

The Purpose of Christians in Recovery®

To bring the Gospel of our Lord Jesus Christ to people seeking recovery and wholeness in their lives.

To minister to those seeking recovery from life's trials, problems, addictions and dysfunctions.

To provide information, tools and resources to those in need of recovery so that balance and order may be restored in their lives.

To promote active discussion of the Bible, the Twelve Steps of Christians-in-Recovery® and personal experiences in recovery so that people can come closer to God, become stronger in Him, and be spiritually nourished.

To provide an atmosphere where recovering people may feel comfortable sharing their Christian faith.

To encourage mutual sharing of strength, hope and faith in the Lord Jesus Christ as it pertains to recovery.

To attract others to a belief in God, Jesus Christ and the Holy Spirit as well as recovery.

Programs & Services Offered

Christians in Recovery is an organization which provides information, referral and resources for anyone who is in recovery or who desires to recover from abuse, family dysfunction, depression, anxiety, grief, stress, etc. and/or addictions of alcohol, drugs, food, gambling, pornography, etc. Join with your fellow Christians in recovery and become a member of our Online Community today!

You can also help by making a donation:
https://christians-in-recovery.org/Give

On average, CIR receives 75-100 requests per day for recovery information, referrals and resources are received via telephone, the Internet, fax, e-mail and the US Postal Service. These requests are filled immediately at no charge. It is estimated that in the past year Christians in Recovery has assisted over one-million people all at no charge to them. If a recovery need arises, we are **available online to help** from 8:00AM until 11:00PM Eastern Time every day, 7 days a week.

We provide a **Christian Online Community** that is rich in content and helps our members grow spiritually. Three separate, comprehensive web sites that require daily maintenance and updating are administered. These sites contain over three-thousand pages of information and resources for Christians, recovering people and their families:

http://christians-in-recovery.org

We are not supported by any group, organization or denomination. We are supported *solely* by people like you who become members or donate. Christians in Recovery is a 501(c)(3) nonprofit organization. All donations are tax deductible to the extent allowed by law.

We offer supporting members of our community **Message Boards** and **Chat Rooms** to further their recovery walk, enhance the Christian recovery community and help people to grow spiritually. For a full description of membership benefits see:

http://Christians-in-Recovery.org/Membership_Benefits

Recovery and Bible related software is written and distributed to assist those who are in recovery or seeking recovery as well as those who work with the recovery community such as counselors, pastors, ministers, etc. Information on this may be found here:

http://self-helpsoftware.com

RecoveryBooks.com, our online bookstore was opened in 1997 and offers thousands of recovery, Christian and self-help titles (at a discount) which people can browse and buy. This bookstore is found here:

http://RecoveryBooks.com

This is available to everyone who seeks it 24 hours a day, every day of the week. In addition, Christians in Recovery writes and distributes its own informational books on recovery.

The Twelve Steps of Christians In Recovery®

1

We admitted we were powerless over our addictions and dysfunctions — that our lives had become unmanageable.

2

Came to believe that a Power greater than ourselves could restore us to sanity and stability.

3

Made a decision to turn our will and our lives over to the care of God, as revealed in the Bible.

4

Made a searching and fearless moral inventory of ourselves.

5

Admitted to God, to ourselves and to another human being the exact nature of our wrongs.

6

Were entirely ready to have God remove all these defects of character.

7

Humbly asked Him to remove our shortcomings.

8

Made a list of all persons we had harmed and became willing to make amends to them all.

9

Made direct amends to such people whenever possible, except when to do so would injure them or others.

10

Continued to take personal inventory and when we were wrong promptly admitted it.

11

Sought through Prayer and Meditation to improve our conscious contact with God, as revealed in the Bible, praying only for knowledge of His will for us and the power to carry that out.

12

Having had a spiritual awakening as a result of these steps, we tried to carry this message to others, and to practice these principles in all our affairs.

Note: The Twelve Steps are reprinted with permission of Alcoholics Anonymous World Services, Inc. Permission to reprint and adapt the Twelve Steps does not mean that AA is affiliated with this program in any way, shape or form. The Twelve Steps are reprinted with permission of Alcoholics Anonymous World Services, Inc. A.A. is a program of recovery from alcoholism only - use of the Twelve Steps in connection with programs and activities which are patterned after A.A., but which address other problems, or in any other non-A.A. context, does not imply otherwise. Additionally, although A.A. is a spiritual program, it is not a religious program. Hence, A.A. is not allied with any sect, denomination or specific spiritual belief.

The Twelve Steps of Alcoholics Anonymous

1. We admitted we were powerless over alcohol, that our lives had become unmanageable.

2. Came to believe that a power greater than ourselves could restore us to sanity.

3. Made a decision to turn our will and our lives over to the care of God, as we understood Him.

4. Made a searching and fearless moral inventory of ourselves.

5. Admitted to God, to ourselves and to another human being the exact nature of our wrongs.

6. Were entirely ready to have God remove these defects of character.

7. Humbly asked Him to remove our shortcomings.

8. Made a list of all persons we had harmed and became willing to make amends to them all.

9. Made direct amends to such people whenever possible, except when to do so would injure them or others.

10. Continued to take personal inventory, and when we were wrong promptly admitted it.

11. Sought through prayer and meditation to maintain our conscious contact with God, *as we understood Him*, praying only for knowledge of His will for us and the power to carry that out.

12. Having had a spiritual awakening as a result of these steps, we tried to carry this message to alcoholics, and to practice these principles in all our affairs.

The Amplified Serenity Prayer

God [Almighty, all loving, all knowing Redeemer] grant [give, provide, impart to] me the serenity [peace of mind, tranquility] to accept [willingly receive] the things I cannot [am unable to] change [alter, modify] the Courage [bravery, strength] to change the things (events, conditions, thoughts) I can, and the Wisdom [knowledge, insight] to know [understand, acknowledge, recognize] the difference;

Living one day at a time (keeping things simple, living one hour or minute at a time if need be); Accepting [bearing, enduring] hardship [adversity, suffering] as a pathway to peace [serenity, peace of mind, tranquility]; Taking, as Jesus (my Lord and my Savior) did, this sinful [ungodly, wicked, unholy] world as it is, not as I would have it (would like it to be): Trusting [believing, being confident] that you (my Heavenly Father) will make all things right (as they should be) if I surrender to [yield to, acquiesce, accept] your will [plan for my life] (perfection of purpose); that I may be reasonably happy [satisfied, fulfilled, joyous] in this life and supremely [completely, altogether, totally, entirely] happy [satisfied, fulfilled, joyous] with you forever [eternally, everlastingly] in the next.

Suggested Format for Twelve-Step Recovery Meeting

It's important to note that our meetings are designed to provide a safe haven for Christians in many kinds of recovery. We earnestly strive to provide a warm and Christian atmosphere. Problems that are too personal to share with more than one person may be taken to a private chat room and discussed with Jesus as the only other Witness.

We make it a point to respect the faiths and beliefs of others, and our meetings are in no way a platform for debating the faith of another or their beliefs. CIR looks for the commonality we all share through Jesus Christ.

We ask that you refrain from giving advice, unless it is asked for, and please do not be judgmental of others, no matter what they have to share. Let others validate their emotions by sharing them, and please never interrupt the speaker with anything that will detract from their chain of comments. Common courtesy is very important to us.

The following format is highly recommended to facilitate God's Purpose, while maintaining a non-denominational atmosphere.

Prayer
Open the meeting with prayer, asking God to open your hearts and minds to receive His Word.

A Welcome & Opening Remarks
Welcome members and guests. Introduce any new persons or visitors. Each meeting is opened in prayer by either the Host or any member in attendance. Announcements may be made at this time.

Pre-Topic Posting
Ask members if anyone has a burning desire, or wants to share something on their mind. Members and hosts need to raise their hand to speak. When meeting online, this is done by typing an exclamation-point in their dialogue box (!). They are then acknowledged by the host and given the floor. If no one elects to share, then the main topic is posted.

Topic-Posting
After the opening format, the Host will then announce the Topic for Discussion. This is usually taken from scripture and applied to recovery. It can deal with ANY aspect of recovery and should not be too long. Perhaps list a passage of scripture, followed by a question relating to it and recovery.

Testimonies
Members should then be encouraged to share. Again, when meeting online, members must raise their hand to begin (!). Members are then able to glean and share their understanding of

the topic and how it relates to them and their recovery. Shares have no time limits, and should usually last from 3-10 minutes, depending on the speaker's passion. Upon completing their discourse (concerning online discussions), they must then type the word <Done>. This keeps the format clean without the distraction of cross-talk.

Closing Prayer

The Host usually concludes the meeting in prayer, but someone else may volunteer to lead it. Members may linger and chat as long as they like following a meeting, in either one of the Meeting Rooms or the Lobby.

These recovery meetings are intended to be a safe place for people to share thoughts, troubles, strengths, needs, etc. The more you give to the meetings, the more you will receive in return. All sharing in the group must be kept confidential. Be aware if someone is trying to monopolize the meeting, but trying to contradict others or possessing an argumentative tone. Everyone should feel safe and welcome here.

For more detailed information on starting a Christian in recovery ministry and conducting meetings, please purchase the CD of this Workbook:

http://Self-HelpSoftware.com/Workbook

Extensive information and tips are available there.

Helpful Hints & Closing Suggestions

Our relationship with Jesus Christ and the Heavenly Father is the core of the organization; it is therefore encouraged to share in prayer when we feel the need for the Holy Spirit. We find that prayer not only strengthens those present, it helps us to accept the things we hear and may disagree with. We gladly accept prayer requests at any time, and if someone becomes silent or at a loss for words, a prayer is always the best remedy.

Tips for Leaders

Difference of opinion may arise concerning scripture and/or controversial subjects. Should any type of dissention begin to develop, please stop the whole train of dialogue and take a moment to pray together for unity. We are not here to fight or squabble, but to praise Jesus and ask for His help in our recovery. Please avoid subjects which tend to spark a controversy or denominational rift. Leaders should stay alert for the warning signs of conflict and gently lead the subject back to scripture or the topic at hand. For Jesus Himself tells us not to "engage in foolish arguments over words."

Sponsorship

By utilizing these formats, we have the opportunity to become involved in one of the most basic of God's Ministries, namely the "ministry of encouragement." One way we do this is by sponsoring new persons who may (or may not) be new at practicing the Christian faith. This consists of praying for them and with them, seeing that they attend meetings, encouraging them to read the Word, establishing and maintaining telephone contact with them, and just being available for spiritual insight and encouragement whenever the need arises. This does not mean becoming spiritually and/or financially responsible for that person; we were not formed to enable bad habits or behavior. But sponsoring others in recovery is a responsibility, and is an important part of our recovery, as well as our sponsee's. You do not have to be a "perfect" or model Christian; just someone to lend an ear or offer support.

How to Use This Workbook

This workbook is organized by topic to help you in times of need. It is not intended to be completed from start to finish; rather, it is meant to address those areas of your life which need strengthening at any particular time. Perhaps you are struggling with "Honesty." Simply look up the topic. Perhaps you are struggling with your "New Beginning;" again, look up that particular topic.

Accompanying each topic you will find helpful scripture. When writing down your thoughts, be sure to date them. This is important. As we grow in our spirituality, we will notice that our previous answers begin to change as we change. THAT'S OKAY! Change is exactly what we are looking for!

We strongly recommend that you pray earnestly before beginning any part of this book. Ask God for direction. A good example-prayer might be:

"Dear Heavenly Father, I come before you this day to ask for guidance and discernment as I use this tool of learning. Open my eyes to Your possibilities. Fill me with your Holy Spirit that I may become truly free, experiencing joy and Your peace which surpasses all understanding. In the Name of Jesus I pray. Amen."

Note: Scripture marked "KJV" is from the Authorized King James Version of the Bible. Scripture marked "Weymouth" is from the Weymouth New Testament in Modern Speech.

Take your time and, above all, have fun!

You are doing this with yourself, for yourself, and before God!

Part 1: New Beginnings

Thoughts before Beginning

Let us begin this segment with a reading from scripture, followed by some very personal questions you should ask yourself as you begin this journey:

Proverbs 4:26-27: KJV
"Ponder the path of thy feet, and let all thy ways be established. Turn not to the right hand nor the left; remove thy foot from evil."

Are you in need of a new beginning?

Are you in need of a renewal in your recovery?

Can today be THE DAY for ending a negative habit or starting a positive one to grow within?

How can you actively invite the Power of God to move into your heart and lead you to take action?

Are you struggling to overcome, or do you view yourself as being in a divine relationship with the One with Whom all things are possible?

Are you approaching New Beginnings with an open heart and an open mind?

Part 1: Lesson 1
Abstinence-vs-Recovery

Galatians 5:1 KJV:
"Stand fast therefore in the liberty wherewith Christ hath made us free, and be not entangled again with the yoke of bondage."

There is a vast difference between Abstinence (stopping the use of our addictive substance and/or dysfunctional behavior) and a Lifestyle of Recovery. Recovery means active involvement in a program of personal growth—a whole new Lifestyle. It means recovering from the ongoing effects of addiction on the mind, emotions, body and soul. It means reconnecting with the human race, rebuilding damaged relationships and developing positive friendships. And, most importantly, Recovery means living in a Growing Relationship with God.

Now you need to ask yourself some specific questions regarding this information. After presenting these questions to yourself, please record your answers in the spaces provided in the following pages. Be as detailed and specific as you can. This is an exercise of personal honesty. Address the questions on the following page:

Do you think there is a difference between **Abstinence and Recovery?** *Please explain in the area provided below:*

How has your addiction or dysfunction affected your **Mind and Emotions?** *Please explain here:*

How has your addiction / dysfunction affected your **Body?** *Please explain here:*

How has your addiction / dysfunction affected you **Spiritually?** *Please explain here:*

Are you currently working to **rebuild** *broken or damaged* **relationships?** *If YES, please list how. If NO, please list why:*

Part 1: Lesson 2
Overcoming Abuse and Learning to Trust God

Psalm 34: 18-19

"The Lord is nigh unto them that are of a broken heart; and saveth such as be of a contrite spirit. Many are the afflictions of the righteous. But the Lord delivereth them out of them all."

Many of us have experienced abuse in some shape or form. But it's important to understand Religious Abuse and the impact it may have on us. Religious abuse usually stems from people trying to force-feed us something dogmatic or specifically tailored from doctrine, usually from a particular denomination and viewpoint. In other words, we are told we must jump through certain hoops in order to become the person God wants us to become, or to be saved. Every kind of addictive persona carries a guilt or shame-complex. We are always trying to achieve a sense of normalcy, but due to the baggage of religious abuse and misunderstanding, we never achieve this. We feel powerless to live up to someone else's standards. This failure triggers still more shame and guilt, and this triggers our addictive behavior used to medicate our shame / guilt. As mentioned in the Steps, it's important to turn to the care of God "as we understand Him."

Below is a series of personal questions we must ask ourselves regarding this lesson. Each question has an area provided for your answer.

In what ways have you experienced religious abuse? Please explain below:

How did this affect how you feel about God and your faith?

Are you learning to move beyond religion toward a more Spiritual relationship with Christ?

Do you believe that God wants a personal relationship with you? Why, or why not?

Do you want a personal relationship with God? Why, or why not?

Please list what you think may be hindering that closer bond with God?

Do you feel unworthy of His grace and mercy? Do you feel fearful or doubtful of His Love? Please explain why.

Part 1: Lesson 3
Abuse-vs-Unconditional Love

Luke 6:27-29 KJV:

"But I say unto you which hear, Love your enemies, do good to them which hate you, Bless them that curse you, and pray for them that despitefully use you. And unto him that smiteth thee on the one cheek offer also the other; and him that taketh away thy coat forbid not to take thy coat also. "

Unconditional Love can be difficult to understand at best. Let us look at this infinite example of God's Love and see how we can expand our personal borders concerning our limited forms of conditional love.

How does God expect us to love someone or something we have never met or do not know? This may require some deep and soulful thought. Record your thoughts here:

Are you able to love unconditionally despite what others do to you?

What is the difference between unconditional love and allowing yourself to be abused?

Do you have boundaries which you set? Please list what they are here:

Relate an experience of yours that is a good example of where you are with unconditional love and abuse:

Part 1: Lesson 4
Accountability

Luke 12:48 KJV
"For unto whomsoever much is given, of him shall be much required."

The way to recovery is through accountability. When we blow-it, we have to admit it. By admitting and confessing we place a marker down. We stand on that marker and use it as a place to move forward from. If we do not admit (confess), no marker is in place and we cannot move forward.

Are you accountable to anyone? If yes, please explain why. If no, why not?

Do you feel accountable to God?

How often do you check-in with God?

How does Accountability factor into your recovery?

How is your recovery without Accountability? Please give detailed answer:

What have you learned about Accountability today?

Part 1: Lesson 5
Making Amends to Others

Luke 6:36-38 KJV

"Be ye therefore merciful, as your Father also is merciful. Judge not, and ye shall not be judged: condemn not, and ye shall not be condemned: forgive, and ye shall be forgiven: Give, and it shall be given unto you; good measure, pressed down, and shaken together, and running over, shall men give into your bosom. For with the same measure that ye mete withal it shall be measured to you again."

In making Amends we quickly learn that different people and situations can require different and unique approaches. Some need to be approached as soon as possible so we can get moving forward with our lives. At times, however, there are some which make this difficult. This may be because they are not trustworthy or do not maintain our confidence. With these people, we may only want to achieve a partial amends at first, before going on to make full amends. With others, we may need to leave it at a partial amends and be done with it. With others still, it is completely impossible to even approach them with words. As Christians we are to love our enemies, bless those who curse us, and pray for those who use us for personal gain. In making amends, we must move above our human emotions and approach them with love in our hearts, just as Jesus had done.

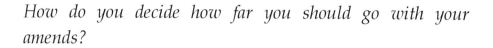

How do you decide how far you should go with your amends?

Can being impatient to make amends cause more damage than good? Have you ever experienced this?

What is the difference between merely apologizing and making a true amends?

What difficulties do you have when making amends with those who bear a grudge against you, one founded on resentment from the past?

Please explain how we should overcome these difficulties and successfully deal with them as Christians in recovery.

What have you learned from making amends to others today?

Part 1: Lesson 6
Making Amends to God and to Yourself

Jeremiah 31:34

"For I will forgive their iniquity, and I will remember their sin no more."

When making amends, we often think of repairing our relationships with others. But it is even more important to make amends with yourself before God. Let the Lord know of your contrition surrounding your addictive behavior. Let Him know you are sorry and ask His forgiveness.

Have you made amends with yourself? How did you achieve this? How will you achieve this?

What aspect of yourself needs amending? Do you need to make a physical, psychological or spiritual amends?

Why is it harder making amends to yourself than others? If so, why?

Have you made direct amends with God? How did you accomplish this? If not, how WILL you accomplish this?

What have you learned about the types of amends today?

Part 1: Lesson 7
Dealing with Anger

James 1:19-20 KJV

"Let every man be swift to hear, slow to speak, slow to wrath. The wrath of man worketh not the righteousness of God."

We all get angry over a variety of things. Someone is pushing our buttons, or something did not go our way. But overt expressions of anger are not only destructive to us, but everyone around us. Yet keeping anger pent-up can be equally destructive, causing everything from headaches to high blood-pressure.

How do you express your anger? Please be specific:

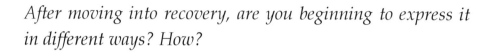

After moving into recovery, are you beginning to express it in different ways? How?

If you really want to "throttle" someone, what can you do to avoid doing so?

Please list some appropriate ways of dealing with anger here:

What do feel is appropriate scripture to help you guide yourself through anger?

Part 1: Lesson 8
Devising a Battle Plan

Ephesians 6:11-12 KJV

"Put on the whole armor of God, that ye may be able to stand against the wiles of the devil. For we wrestle not against flesh and blood, but against principalities, against powers, against the rulers of the darkness of this world, against spiritual wickedness in high places."

"A plan must be laid. A commitment must be made. A price must be paid." –Robert Schuller

No war was ever won unless the many individual battles were successful. In order to succeed in battle, we must devise a successful battle plan. You should be able to easily name the specifics of your plan and be willing to share it with others. Get a fresh pad of paper and a pen, or start a new file. Be as elaborate as you want with your plan, and even place in contingencies. Be ready to go around obstacles. Your plan should be fluent and best fitted to what you would define as God's Will for you. Please see next page for questions.

Have you devised a battle plan for yourself and your recovery? Discuss it with yourself here:

Explain the details of your Battle Plan here. Get it down on paper, save it to your computer, and be ready to share any aspect of it with others. We all need Battle Plans and aspects of yours may help another with theirs. If you have NOT formed a Battle Plan, do so now:

Have you made a commitment to God in your Plan?

Have you made a commitment to Yourself?

Have you made a commitment to your Sponsor?

Exactly what are these commitments? Please list them here:

What price have you paid for not having a plan?

Are you paying a price now?

Does living in Recovery seem worth the price? If so, list here. If not, please explain:

Part 1: Lesson 9
Be Still

Psalm 46:10
"Be still, and know that I am God."

Learning to reside in a state of peace is an important part of the recovery process. This is a period when the noise and dissonance is moved aside so we can breathe freely and easily in His Presence. This is commonly known as **Serenity.**

How can you learn to be still, giving yourself "permission" to relax and slow down?

Is it hard for you to be still? Why?

Why is it hard for you to find inner-serenity?

What steps do you take to prepare yourself for a still and relaxed mindset?

Part 1: Lesson 10
Destruction-vs-Conviction

2 Corinthians 7:9-10

"Now I rejoice, not in your grief, but because the grief led to repentence., for you sorrowed with a Godly sorrow, which prevented you from receiving injury from us in any respect. For Godly sorrow produces Repentance leading to Salvation; a repentance not to be regretted; but the sorrow of the world finally produces death."

Realizing that our time here on earth is merely a stage in our spiritual development is an important realization. If you have sinned, pray for forgiveness, and pray with your heart. The light of forgiveness and salvation will set you free. You will find yourself on entirely new spiritual footing.

What is the difference between the devil's accusations about your past, and the convictions of the Holy Spirit regarding forgiveness?

How do you discern the difference between the two? How will you recognize them when taking a moral inventory?

How do you eliminate the accusations while gaining new convictions? How to you prevent accusations from continuously rattling around your head?

Part 1: Lesson 11
Embracing Change

Romans 12:2

"And be not conformed to this world: but be ye transformed by the renewing of your mind, that ye may prove what is the good, and acceptable, and perfect will of God."

Some people have been in recovery for years, while others are just starting out. But the time spent in recovery has no bearing on the quality of changes which will happen, both large and small. Before recovery, you were the captain of your own ship, doing the piloting until you found yourself in a disastrous wreck. In recovery you must unreservedly and wholeheartedly allow Jesus to pilot your vessel through the shoals and storms of life. In the end, your voyage will be rewarding and fulfilling.

What changes have taken place in you since beginning recovery?

What changes have taken place since your surrendered your will and your life over to the care of God?

Why are these changes important to you? Be as thorough and descriptive as possible.

Part 1: Lesson 12
Releasing the Burden of Self

Matthew 12: 24-26

"Then said Jesus unto His disciples, 'If any man will come after Me, let him deny himself and take up his cross, and follow me. For whosoever will save his life shall lose it: and whosoever shall lose his life for My sake shall find it. For what is a man profited if he should win the entire world and lose his own soul? Or what shall a man give in exchange for his soul?'"

AA Prayer (AA Big Book, P.63)

"God, I offer thyself to Thee — To build with me and to do with me as Thou will. Relieve me of the bondage of Self, that I may better do Thy will."

We should begin every new day with a prayer asking for release of the Self. Let us see the world through unbiased, corrupt or sinful eyes, without Original Sin blocking our view. This is my personal prayer:

"Dear Lord, I humbly come before You this day asking that You grant me another day of recovery. Release me from the bondage of Self that I may do Your will, not mine, this day. Thank You for my gift for wholeness. In Jesus' Name I pray, Amen."

How does the Burden of Self try to spoil or impede your plans of recovery?

Do you consider yourself overly self-serving or self-centered? What is the difference between willfully attaining your needs and being selfish?

Who, or what, came first in your life prior to recovery?

Who, or what, comes first now? Why?

Are you still struggling with the Burden of Self? Please note how?

How can you change this?

Part 1: Lesson 13
Child of God

1John 4:7-13 Weymouth

"Dear friends, let us love one another, for love has its origin in God, and everyone who loves has become a child of God and is beginning to know God. He who is destined to love has never had any knowledge of God; because God is Love.

"God's love for us has been manifested in that He has sent His only Son into the world so that we may have Life through Him. This is love indeed – we did not love God, but He loved us and sent His Son to be an atoning sacrifice for our sins.

"Dear friends, if God has so loved us, we also ought to love one another. No one has ever yet seen God. If we love one another, God continues in union with us, and His love with all its perfection is in our hearts. We can know tat we are continuing in union with Him and that He is continuing in union with us, by the fact that He has given us a portion of His Spirit. And we have seen and bear witness that the Father has sent the Son to be the Savior of the world."

Romans 8: 16

"The spirit itself beareth witness with our spirit, that we are the children of God."

The next time someone reminds you of a mistake or failure from your past, telling you that you will never be worth anything, tell them that you are a child of God. Tell them that every sin you have ever committed is under the Blood of Jesus never to be remembered or held against you again. Tell them that Jesus is able to present you faultless and with exceeding joy to Himself. Indeed, our precious Savior is able to do anything.

Jude 1:24-25

"Now unto him that is able to keep you from falling, and to present you faultless before the presence of His glory with exceeding joy. To the only wise God, our Savior, be glory and majesty, dominion and power, both now and forever. Amen."

Why is it important to become a child of God?

How does one become a child of God?

What would you tell someone who did not feel worthy of being a child of God?

What does it mean to become a part of God's Family, and how does this change your life?

Part 1: Lesson 14
Death of Self

John 12:24-26 Weymouth

"In most solemn truth I tell you that unless the grain of wheat falls into the ground and dies, it remains what it was — a single grain; but that if it dies it yields a rich harvest. He who holds his life dear, is destroying it; and he who makes his life of no account in this world, shall keep it to the Life of Ages.

"If a man wishes to be my servant let him follow me; and where I am, so too will my servant be. If a man wishes to be my servant, the father will honor him."

Placing our focus on the will of God, rather than our own limited views and selfish will, is a vital part of the recovery process. We must turn our will over to our Creator and we will discover that raw, destructive emotions are removed from much of our life.

How can you apply the above scripture to your recovery?

What does it mean when Jesus says if you love your life you will lose it, and if you detach from earthly desire, you will keep it?

What can you do today to follow Christ more closely and serve Him?

What is the difference between believing in God and KNOWING Him?

Part 1: Lesson 15
Developing Discipline

Luke 9: 62 KJV

"And Jesus said unto him, 'No man, having put his hand to the plow, and looking back, is fit for the Kingdom of God.'"

As soon as we have it made in recovery, as soon as we start getting comfortable with where we are in lives, we start getting lazy. Proper attention is not devoted to the maintenance of life's day-to-day cycle.

Recovery can be similar to balancing our checkbooks. Hardly anyone likes to do it. A lot of us hate every second of the procedure. But it must be done to keep things under control and prevent financial chaos. Whenever we begin to neglect updating our checkbook, things can spiral out of hand in rather short order. Recovery is much the same.

Are you lacking discipline in any part of your recovery? What are you having trouble getting under control about yourself?

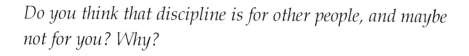

Do you think that discipline is for other people, and maybe not for you? Why?

Do you lack discipline to maintain the momentum needed for certain things to succeed?

Write about an incident in your recovery when you got lazy in any aspect of your recovery, and the consequences:

What are the steps you use to snap yourself back into line?

Do you have a solid routine of daily maintenance? Please describe this routine. If not, please devise one here:

Why should you make such an effort to devise a daily routine of recovery?

What have you learned about discipline today?

Part 1: Lesson 16
The Leap of Faith

Matthew 17: 20

"Verily I say to you, if ye have faith as the grain of a mustard seed, ye shall say unto this mountain, Remove hence to yonder place; and it shall remove; and nothing shall be impossible to you."

A leap of faith is not a one-time thing. We must be ready to continually take this leap as we place our hope trust in God. Our leaps will begin to encompass greater and greater distances.

Do you understand the above-phrase from scripture? What does it mean to you?

Write about your first experience at taking a leap of faith:

What do you remember most about it?

Do you think God is asking you to take a leap of faith about any present circumstance in your life? Please write about it:

Part 1: Lesson 17
When the Family is Made Sick

Genesis 3:6

"And when the woman saw that the tree was good for food, and that it was pleasant to the eyes, and a tree to be desired to make one wise, she took of the fruit thereof, and did eat, and gave also unto her husband with her; and he did eat."

No matter what the addiction or dysfunction, in the end we realize that it is a disease that affects not just us, but anyone associated with us, including family, friends, co-workers and neighbors.

When did you first realize that your addiction/dysfunction was a matter involving your entire family? Talk about who was affected, and what the direct affects were:

Could you clearly see your role in it? How?

What exactly led you to this realization?

How did it make you feel?

What did you do to try to fix the situation?

Part 1: Lesson 18

Fear

2Timothy 1:7 KJV

"For God hath not given us the spirit of fear; but of power, and of love, and of a sound mind."

We all have fears and they can be quite debilitating at times. Often we try to deny, hide or mask our fears by indulging in our addiction or dysfunction. This tends to make things even worse. Like a fly on flypaper, the harder we struggle the more stuck we become. Be specific about what is helping you, eg: that scripture verse, phrase in the Big Book or other recovery book, recovery thought, or facet of your faith.

Is there a reoccurring fear in your life that is plaguing you, a fear that has you by the throat and won't let go? What it is that you fear?

How do you feel about this fear? Does it fill you with anger, fright, shame, self-pity, remorse, resentment, pain or anguish?

Why does it continue to haunt you?

Is your life unmanageable because of this fear?

Is your faith, scripture and the Twelve Steps helping you to deal with it? Why or why not? Please explain here:

Part 1: Lesson 19
God's Standards

Ephesians 5:8 KJV

"For ye were sometimes darkness, but now are ye light in the LORD: walk as children of light."

Before becoming a Christian in recovery we appraise ourselves according to our own standards. In recovery, we begin to apply God's standards to our lives. Things that used to be acceptable, gradually become intolerable. We no longer hope things change. We make the changes.

What do you feel are God's standards for you?

Are you able to live up to them? Why or why not?

What areas of your life need more work?

What do you intend to do about it?

Part 1: Lesson 20
Grace of God (Part A)

Titus 3:3-7 Weymouth

"For there was a time when we also were deficient in understanding, obstinate, deluded, the slaves of various cravings and pleasures, spending our lives in malice and envy, hateful ourselves and hating one another. But when the goodness of God our Savior, and His love to man, dawned upon us, not in consequence of things which we, as righteous men, had done, but as the result of His own mercy He saved us by means of the bath of regeneration and the renewal of our natures by the Holy Spirit, which He poured out on us richly through Jesus Christ our Savior; in order that having been declared righteous through His grace we might become heirs to the Life of the Ages in fulfillment of our hopes."

Do not assume that temptations which have defeated you in the past will continue to do so. In recovery, temptation is opportunity — opportunity to tap into the power of the Holy Spirit and overcome, opportunity to increase God's good hand upon your life. The power of the Holy Spirit should be felt in our lives in very practical ways. God never gives us tasks equal to our power. He gives us power equal to our tasks.

Do you feel you have been reborn or renewed by the Holy Spirit?

What does the Grace of God mean to you?

When did you first become aware of God's Grace?

What impact has it had on your faith in God?

What impact has it had on your daily walk as a Christian?

Do you feel that Christ has intervened in your life or taken an active part in your recovery?

*Are you different now than you were previously?
How have you changed?*

What have you learned about the Grace of God today?

Part 1: Lesson 21
Grace of God (Part B)

Romans 3:22-26 Weymouth

"For all alike have sinned, and all consciously come short of the glory of God, gaining acquittal from guilt by His free un-purchased grace through the deliverance which is found in Christ Jesus. He it is whom God put forward as a Mercy-seat, rendered efficacious through faith in His blood, in order to demonstrate His righteousness--because of the passing over, in God's forbearance, of the sins previously committed-- with a view to demonstrating, at the present time, His righteousness, that He may be shown to be righteous Himself, and the giver of righteousness to those who believe in Jesus.

"In matters of grace, we all have Benjamin's portion – we all have ten times more than we expected! And though our necessities are great – yet are we often amazed at the marvelous plenty of grace, which God gives us experimentally to enjoy." –Charles Spurgeon

"All God's blessings go together, like links in a golden chain. If He gives converting grace, He will also give comforting grace. He will send 'showers of blessing.' 'Look up today, O parched plant – and open your leaves and flowers for a heavenly watering.'"
--Charles Spurgeon

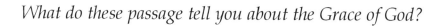

What do these passage tell you about the Grace of God?

Have you personally experienced the Grace of God in your life--your recovery? If so, write about it. If not, express your feelings about not having experienced it.

Part 1: Lesson 22
Grace vs. Human Effort

Ephesians 4:7 KJV
"But unto every one of us is given grace according to the measure of the gift of Christ."
2 Corinthians 9:6 KJV
"But this I say, He which soweth sparingly shall reap also sparingly; and he which soweth bountifully shall reap also bountifully."

How confusing it is to try and balance the truth between God's grace and human effort. We often depend too much on ourselves and yet "depend" too much on the type of thinking that "God will do it all". Neither is correct.

How do you keep a proper balance in your recovery between doing things on your own power and Letting Go and Letting God?

What signs do you look for that it is up to you to take action?

How do you know when things should be left totally in the hands of God?

When do you know it should be a joint effort?

Share any other thoughts you have on this topic as well as scripture that speaks to you regarding this.

Part 1: Lesson 24
Grief

Psalm 34: 18-19 KJV

"The LORD [is] nigh unto them that are of a broken heart; and saveth such as be of a contrite spirit. {unto...: Heb. to the broken of heart} {of a contrite...: Heb. contrite of spirit} Many [are] the afflictions of the righteous: but the LORD delivereth him out of them all."

"In all our weaknesses, we may rest on His strength. In all our sorrow, we may rest on His sympathy. In all our perplexity, we may rest on His guidance. In all our need, we may rest on His help. I all our danger, we may rest on His deliverance."
--Newman Hall, *Leaves of Healing from the Garden Grief*

What loss in your life have you not fully grieved for?

How does this affect you and your recovery?

Do you feel that you can deal with grief adequately? Why or why not?

Part 1: Lesson: 24
Hate and Love

John 13:35-35 KJV

"A new commandment I give unto you, That ye love one another; as I have loved you, that ye also love one another. By this shall all men know that ye are My disciples, if ye have love one to another."

Hatred is like a cancer that eats us from the inside-out. The object of our hatred feels nothing. Yet all the while we are slowly and surely destroying our own selves.

Are there still people/things you actively hate?

Do you think it's possible to love and hate at the same time?

How does hate relate to your addiction, codependency and/or recovery?

Describe the role of love in your addiction, codependency and/or recovery?

What is your responsibility as a Christian concerning hate?

What is your responsibility as a Christian regarding love?

Part 1: Lesson 25
Honesty - No More Secrets

Romans 13:13-14 KJV

"Let us walk honestly, as in the day; not in rioting and drunkenness, not in chambering and wantonness, not in strife and envying. But put ye on the Lord Jesus Christ, and make not provision for the flesh, to fulfill the lusts thereof."

AA Big Book: *"We took stock honestly.....We went back through our lives. Nothing counted but thoroughness and honesty.....We admitted our wrongs honestly and were willing to set these matters straight."*

How honest are you to yourself regarding your addiction / dysfunction?

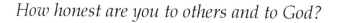

How honest are you to others and to God?

*Have you **really** come clean? Are you still dishonest about your addiction/dysfunction? Why? It is out of Shame or Fear?*

Part 1: Lesson 26
Impatience in Recovery

James 1:4-6 KJV
"But let patience have her perfect work, that ye may be perfect and entire, wanting nothing. If any of you lack wisdom, let him ask of God, that giveth to all men liberally, and upbraideth not; and it shall be given him. But let him ask in faith, nothing wavering."

We tend to view recovery with a worldly perception rather than the way God does. God wants more than recovery, He wants restoration and wholeness. Traditional recovery says, "Take Steps 1-12 and you will be recovered. This also encourages us to put a worldly framework and timetable around recovery. We get angry and frustrated with God when we have followed steps 1,2,3 and still have our addictions/dysfunction. Thus, we play right into the enemy's hand. Also, by thinking we can analyze our recovery, this also gives us the impression that we can manipulate the recovery process. We can't put God on a time clock and we can't rush Him. He is eternal...He is outside of time! We are the only ones in time! By taking the worldly "recovery" approach we tend to focus on recovery instead of God. "God when are you going to deliver me from this madness?" Our recovery and addiction/dysfunction can and will become our gods when we place them out front and above God. This is exactly what the enemy wants...idol worship.

Our primary goal should be to be more like Christ and He should be that "light at the end of the tunnel." The concept of "recovery" has become a crutch for some of us. True we talk about God providing us strength and grace but we don't talk about getting to know the source of the strength and grace by sitting at His feet.

What does "recovery" mean to you?

When will you consider yourself "recovered?"

Do you get angry with God because you are not "recovered?" Why?

Do you put a framework and timetable around your recovery?
Explain:

What can you do now (each day) to change your focus from recovery and place it on the ONE who can transform us from glory to glory? (**2 Corinthians 3:18**)

Part 1: Lesson 27
Impossible Made Possible

1 Corinthians 2:9 Weymouth

"...things which eye has not seen nor ear heard, and which have never entered the heart of man: all that God has in readiness for them that love Him."

We have no reason to fear the impossible, for it is God who fights the battle for us. Even when the battles of life seem impossible to win, put your confidence in God who fights, not only **with** you, but **for** you.

Has God brought about something or things in your life that you thought could never happen?

What has come about in your life that, without question, is a gift from God?

What started you on the road to recovery? An event? a person? hitting bottom? Or did God directly intervene in your life? Be specific.

What have you learned about God's Possibilities versus Human Possibilities today?

Part 1: Lesson 28
Letting Go and Letting God

Psalm 37:5 KJV
"Commit thy way unto the LORD; trust also in Him; and He shall bring it to pass."

Proverbs 3:5 KJV
"Trust in the LORD with all thine heart; and lean not unto thine own understanding."

In recovery we soon see the benefits of this healing process. Changes happen that we never imagined and that we never could have achieved on our own. Once we learn to practice getting out of God's way and our own way; Learning to turn the outcome of things over to Him things get easier. God has tremendous goals that he has planned for you and all you need do is put one foot in front of the other. One step at a time. Scripture provides us with a set of spiritual tools so we can get out of the Creator's way and have the ability to do His will in lieu of our own.

In the past, how have you stood in God's way, or your own way?

What does it mean to you to Let Go and Let God?

What changes do you think God has in mind for you?

Can you implicitly trust God for these changes to take place? What goals do you think God wants you to achieve?

Can you make His goals for you, your own goals?

Part 1: Lesson 29
Living with Someone in Active Addiction

Matthew 10:16
"Behold, I am sending you out as sheep in the midst of wolves, so be wise as serpents and innocent as doves."

Many people are living with a spouse or loved one who is active in their addiction and/or dysfunctional behavior. This can be quite trying especially when you have your own addictions / dysfunctions with which you are trying to deal. We must be "wise as serpents" when confronting our loved ones who are actively using.

Write a bit about your current situation:

How do you strike a balance between your own recovery and the needs of this other person or persons?

What are the hardest things you have to deal with?

In what ways are you dealing with it inappropriately?

What do you feel are more appropriate ways?

Part 1: Lesson 30
Loneliness

John 14:16-20 KJV

"And I will pray the Father, and He shall give you another Comforter, that He may abide with you forever; Even the Spirit of truth; whom the world cannot receive, because it seeth Him not, neither knoweth Him: but ye know Him; for He dwelleth with you, and shall be in you. I will not leave you comfortless: I will come to you. Yet a little while, and the world seeth Me no more; but ye see Me: because I live, ye shall live also. At that day ye shall know that I am in my Father, and ye in Me, and I in you."

We have all experienced the inner pain of loneliness despite the fact that we know that Christ is with us always (Matthew 28:20), the Holy Spirit is our Comforter (John 14:16,26), and we have fellowship with one another and God (1 John 1:3-4).

Are you experiencing loneliness now? If so, why?

What can you do about it?

Practically speaking, can God fill the void or does it need to be filled with personal relationships?

What role has loneliness played in your addiction / dysfunction?

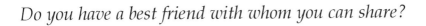

Do you have a best friend with whom you can share?

Is there any scripture that you find comforting in times of loneliness? If so, write it down here.

Part 1: Lesson 31
Needs that are Unfulfilled

Job 6:8
"Oh that I might have my request; and that God would grant me the thing that I long for."

When we really work the Christian life, we sometimes think that by keeping God first in our lives all our needs will be met. Yet we find ourselves needy. Intimacy, companionship and sex are needed from our mates. Other needs are not fulfilled.

Does putting God first in your life mean that you will have no unfulfilled needs?

If you have unfulfilled needs, does that mean you are not "right" with God?

What is the difference between a need and a want, or an addiction / dysfunction?

Do you have a difficult time discerning what you need to allow God to do and what you need to do for yourself? (like the story of the man who was drowning, wanted God to save him, but refused the row boat, the motor boat, the helicopter, died & was angry at God for not rescuing him). Explain here:

Part 1: Lesson 32
Priorities--First things First

Matthew 6:33 KJV
"But seek ye first the kingdom of God, and his righteousness; and all these things shall be added unto you."

A major stumbling block in recovery can be putting one's desire to be free from addictive/dysfunctional behaviors ahead of the desire for God Himself. Priorities somehow become reversed.

List the priorities in your life in the order that you have been living them :

*Now list the priorities as they **should** be in your life*

*What is your absolute **FIRST** priority?*

How do you think these misplaced priorities have detracted from your recovery?

What changes can and will you make?

Part 1: Lesson 33
Recovery Paralysis

Hebrews 12:1-3 Weymouth

"Therefore, surrounded as we are by such a vast cloud of witnesses, let us fling aside every encumbrance and the sin that so readily entangles our feet. And let us run with patient endurance the race that lies before us, simply fixing our gaze upon Jesus, our Prince Leader in the faith, who will also award us the prize. He, for the sake of the joy which lay before Him, patiently endured the cross, looking with contempt upon its shame, and afterwards seated Himself-- where He still sits--at the right hand of the throne of God."

It is so easy in recovery to become paralyzed by the seeming mountain of our problems and apparent precipices of addictive/dysfunctional behavior. They are things that appear to be insurmountable by us.

Do you go to your fellow Christians for the support and encouragement you need? If not, why not? How can you change this?

Can you realistically lay aside every weight and the sin that clings so closely? Why or why not?

Do you look to yourself, your addiction/dysfunction or to Jesus for Strength? Please explain:

Courage?

Peace?

Part 1: Lesson 34
Dealing with the Past

Psalm 51:2, 7, 10 KJV

"Wash me thoroughly from mine iniquity, and cleanse me from my sin. Purge me with hyssop, and I shall be clean: wash me, and I shall be whiter than snow. Create in me a clean heart, O God; and renew a right spirit within me."

When taking inventory we look over our past actions and behavior and the resulting debris in our current lives. We deal with the past and clean our house in order to free ourselves and set out on a new beginning and life in recovery.

Is it possible for you to make a new beginning for yourself without dealing with your past?

Do you feel it is possible to free yourself for ever from your past?

Have you dealt with your past? If not, why are you still struggling with it? What can you do about it?

Do you have a favorite scripture that "says it all" for you regarding inventory and freedom from the past.

Part 1: Lesson 35
Prayer and Meditation

Psalm 19:14 KJV

"Let the words of my mouth, and the meditation of my heart, be acceptable in thy sight, O LORD, my strength, and my redeemer."

Prayer and Meditation are our principal means of conscious contact with God.

Do you pray and/or meditate as much as you think you should?

Do you find it hard to find the time to pray and mediate?

Are you still developing these skills?

In your personal opinion, what is the difference between prayer and meditation?

When is it easiest for you to pray and meditate? When is it most difficult for you?

If someone asked you how to go about prayer and meditation what would you tell them?

What have you learned about Prayer and Meditation Today?

Part 1: Lesson 36
Prayer and Recovery

Psalm 91:15 KJV

"He shall call upon me, and I will answer him: I will be with him in trouble; I will deliver him."

Romans 8:26-28

"Likewise the Spirit also helped our infirmities: for we know not what we should pray for as we ought: but the Spirit itself makes intercession for us with groaning which cannot be uttered. And he that searches the heart knows what is the mind of the Spirit, because He makes intercession for the saints according to the will of God. And we know that all things work together for good to them that love God, to them who are called according to His purpose."

What role does prayer play in your recovery? None? A little? A lot? Why?

Do you find it to be a helpful tool? Please explain why:

When you pray, do you "talk" to God as a loving Father or do you perceive Him as a dominant-almost scary figure?

How do you pray? What do you say regarding your recovery?

Do you have a favorite prayer? If so, share it. Do you use a cherished daily meditation or devotional?

Part 1: Lesson 37
Principles *Before* Personalities

Luke 6:35-38 KJV

"But love ye your enemies, and do good, and lend, hoping for nothing again; and your reward shall be great, and ye shall be the children of the Highest: for He is kind unto the unthankful and to the evil. Be ye therefore merciful, as your Father also is merciful. Judge not, and ye shall not be judged: condemn not, and ye shall not be condemned: forgive, and ye shall be forgiven: Give, and it shall be given unto you; good measure, pressed down, and shaken together, and running over, shall men give into your bosom. For with the same measure that ye mete withal it shall be measured to you again."

The Big Book of AA tells us to place principles before personalities. As Christians, we are to love one another as Christ loves us and we are told to turn the other cheek. When someone rubs you the wrong way or offends you:

How do you normally react?

Do you take it too personally?

Are you overly defensive or overprotective of yourself?

Are you more capable of handling this type of situation in recovery? If so, why? If not, why not?

Have you learned anything about forgiveness and amends from recovery?

Part 1: Lesson 38
Promises

Peter 1: 3-4 KJV

"According as His divine power hath given unto us all things that pertain unto this life and godliness, through the knowledge of Him that hath called us to glory and virtue: Whereby are given unto us exceeding great and precious promises: that by these ye might be partakers of the divine nature, having escaped the corruption that is in the world through lust."

Alcoholics Anonymous (also known as the Big Book) offers us Promises if we follow the 12 steps. The promises are presented as follows: If we are painstaking about this phase of our development, we will be amazed before we are half way through. We are going to know a new freedom and a new happiness. We will not regret the past nor wish to shut the door on it. We will comprehend the word serenity and we will know peace. No matter how far down the scale we have gone, we will see how our experience can benefit others. That feeling of uselessness and self-pity will disappear. We will lose interest in selfish things and gain interest in our fellows. Self-seeking will slip away. Our whole attitude and outlook upon life will change. Fear of people and of economic insecurity will leave us. We will intuitively know how to handle situations which used to baffle us. We will suddenly realize that God is doing for us what we could not do for ourselves. Are these extravagant promises? We think not. They are being fulfilled among us--sometimes quickly, sometimes slowly. They will always materialize if we work for them.

Have the Promises manifested themselves to you?

If so, which ones?

Have you had to work for them?

What are your most favorite promises?

Part 1: Lesson 39
Recovery as a Lifestyle

Zechariah 1:3 KJV
"Turn ye, unto me, sayeth the LORD of hosts, and I will turn unto you."

Prior to learning about recovery, I was very comfortable with my addictions and dysfunctional living. It was like putting on an old comfortable pair of shoes each day even though they were giving me blisters (destroying me). When I first learned about recovery, I thought there is no way I could be comfortable in the recovery lifestyle. I thought I would always crave my old habits and way of living.

Have you found peace and serenity in the recovery way of living?

Or do you still struggle trying to get out of your addictive / dysfunctional lifestyle?

145

If you are still struggling, why do you think you struggle and what do you think you can do about it?

If you no longer struggle, what do you feel is the key to your success in recovery?

If you had some words of wisdom to pass on to someone else seeking recovery, what would you say?

Part 1: Lesson 40
Relationships in Recovery

Mark 12: 30-31, 33

"And thou shall love the Lord thy God with all of thy heart, and with all of thy soul, and with all of thy mind, and with all of thy strength: this is the first commandment. And the second is like, namely this, Thou shall love thy neighbor as thyself. There is none other commandment greater than these.

"And to love Him with all the heart, and with all the understanding, and with all the soul, and with all the strength, and to love his neighbor as himself, is worth more than all the burnt offerings and sacrifices."

When we enter into recovery quite often we find that certain friends or family members:

1) Distrust us because we have "changed"

2) Are a bit afraid of us because of the change

3) Are not sure the change is permanent or for real

The ground rules of the relationships have changed and people are not sure how to react to it. Some relationships will be strong and last through all these changes but the relationships that were based on our dysfunctional behaviors tend to fall apart.

What changes have occurred in your relationship with others as a result of your recovery? (Be specific):

What have you learned from this?

Would you do anything differently if you had a second chance?

Part 1: Lesson 41
Relationship with God and Recovery

Deuteronomy 10:12 KJV
"What doth the LORD thy God require of thee, but to fear the LORD thy God, to walk in all His ways, and to love Him, and to serve the LORD thy God with all thy heart and with all thy soul."

Matthew 22:37-38 KJV
"Jesus said unto him, Thou shalt love the Lord thy God with all thy heart, and with all thy soul, and with all thy mind. This is the first and great commandment."

People tend to judge how much we love God by how far along we are in recovery. The thinking is that if someone is recovered then they must be really close to God and if someone is having trouble with recovery that their relationship with God must not be close. This is untrue. There are many people who are close to God, who love God with all of their mind and spirit but they are still in bondage to drugs, alcohol, sex, gambling, compulsive behaviors, dysfunctional living, bad relationships etc.

What are your thoughts on this?

Have you had the experience of being close to God while yet not in recovery or not doing well in recovery?

How does your relationship with God affect your recovery?

Do you have a favorite scripture that relates to your relationship with God?

Part 1: Lesson 42
Relationship vs. Religion

Colossians 1:26-28 Weymouth

"I have been appointed to serve the Church in the position of responsibility entrusted to me by God for your benefit, so that I may fully deliver God's Message-- the truth which has been kept secret from all ages and generations, but has now been revealed to His people, to whom it was His will to make known how vast a wealth of glory for the Gentile world is implied in this truth--the truth that `Christ is in you, the hope of glory.' Him we preach, admonishing every one and instructing every one, with all possible wisdom, so that we may bring every one into God's presence, made perfect through Christ."

Romans 8:11 Weymouth

"And if the Spirit of Him who raised up Jesus from the dead is dwelling in you, He who raised up Christ from the dead will give Life also to your mortal bodies because of His Spirit who dwells in you."

As humans we tend to turn what should be an exciting personal relationship with God into a religion. We often try to compartmentalize a God that has no bounds. Paul says that Christ not only came to die for you, but that He came to give His LIFE to you. He dwells within you. He LIVES IN YOU and is an integral part of your being.

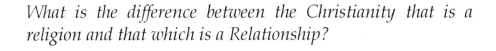

What is the difference between the Christianity that is a religion and that which is a Relationship?

How would you describe this Relationship?

Is your experience with the Religion or the Relationship? Please explain here:

Write down any additional thoughts or scripture that comes to mind:

Part 1: Lesson 43
Resentment

Matthew 7:26-27

"And every one that heareth these sayings of Mine, and doeth them not, shall be likened unto a foolish man, which built his house upon the sand: And the rain descended, and the floods came, and the winds blew, and beat upon that house; and it fell: and great was the fall of it."

In recovery we have to learn to do things God's way and to let go of doing things our way. Many become resentful because: "I can't have things my way, and I can't have things **both** ways because they are mutually exclusive."

Are you resentful because you can no longer have things "your way?" Why?

Has your level of resentment declined with the passage of time?

What is/was "your way?"

What do you feel is "God's way" for you?

Is Gods way the better way or the more painful way for you?

Can you live with the choices you have made? Explain.

Part1: Lesson 44
Responding to God

2 Samuel 22:29 KJV
"For thou art my lamp, O LORD: and the LORD will lighten my darkness."

Luke 1:78-79 KJV
"Through the tender mercy of our God; whereby the dayspring from on high hath visited us, To give light to them that sit in darkness and in the shadow of death, to guide our feet into the way of peace."

God is always present. He is speaking with us. It is up to us to listen, to hear and to respond to Him. He will show us the way. We have to take the steps.

What has God shown you in the past 10 days regarding your Recovery?

How do you think He wants you to respond to this?

*How **will** you respond?*

What have you learned in the past week about your Faith?

Do you think God wants you to do something different?

How will you respond?

Part 1: Lesson 45
Responsibility

1 Corinthians 13:11 KJV

"When I was a child, I spake as a child, I understood as a child, I thought as a child: but when I became a man, I put away childish things."

The bottom line is recovery is, "I am responsible!"

I am responsible for getting my recovery moving again.

I am responsible for the actions I take.

I am responsible for my relationship with God.

Do you take as much responsibility as you **should** *for Your Life, the Actions You Take, Keeping your Recovery Alive and Dynamic every day?*

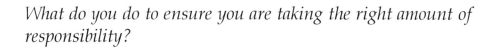

What do you do to ensure you are taking the right amount of responsibility?

What can you do in order to take a more active role in your own recovery?

Part 1: Lesson 46
Resisting Satan

John 8:44 KJV

"...He was a murderer from the beginning, and abode not in the truth, because there is no truth in him. When he speaketh a lie, he speaketh of his own: for he is a liar, and the father of it."

In regards to Satan, the **NIV** says: *"He is a liar and the father of lies."*

Have you ever considered what his lies are?

List some of the lies you feel that Satan has told you or lead you to believe:

How do you discern whether you are hearing lies from Satan, your own thoughts, or direction from God?

How can you most effectively protect yourself from "his fiery darts?"

Include scripture here if you can to support your thoughts on this:

Part 1: Lesson 47
Roadblocks of Recovery

Romans 8:35-39 KJV

"Who shall separate us from the love of Christ? Shall tribulation, or distress, or persecution, or famine, or nakedness, or peril, or sword? For it is written, For Thy sake we are killed all the day long.; we are accounted as sheep for the slaughter. Nay, in all these things we are more than conquers through Him that loved us. For I am persuaded that neither death, nor life, nor angels, nor principalities, nor powers, nor things present, nor things to come, nor height, nor depth, nor any other creature, shall be able to separate us from the love of God, which is in Christ Jesus our Lord."

Realizing that we are never beyond the Love of the Lord is an important part of the recovery process. No matter where we have been, what we have done to others, or what we have done to offend the Lord, He still loves us as if we were His merely misguided child. Turn back to Him and ask for forgiveness with an honest heart.

What is the hardest thing about recovery to you?

What can you do to improve this condition?

Do you believe that God can and will help you? Why? Name some examples in the Bible where God extended a helping hand:

Part 1: Lesson 48
Self Esteem

Isaiah 42:16 KJV

"And I will bring the blind by a way that they knew not; I will lead them in paths that they have not known: I will make darkness light before them, and crooked things straight. These things will I do unto them, and not forsake them."

Most of us enter into recovery with badly damaged self-esteem. It may seem to add insult to injury to have to admit powerlessness over our lives, situations, problems etc. and to come to the realization that our lives are unmanageable.

Has it been a revelation to you to finally admit powerlessness? Please be specific.

What finally brought you to your knees?

Did you feel that God was working in your life at this point or had you given up all hope?

How has your self-esteem and self-image changed as a result of taking Step One?

Is there something in your life now that you are having trouble admitting your powerlessness over?

Part 1: Lesson 49
Selfishness

2 Corinthians 5:15

"And that He died for all, that they which live should not henceforth live unto themselves, but unto Him which died for them, and rose again."

We do not think of ourselves as selfish until we begin to learn what addiction and dysfunctional living is all about. It is only when we start to take an honest and hard look at our behaviors that selfishness comes to light.

Do you feel you have been selfish? If so, what bearing did it have on your behavior?

So what is wrong with selfishness anyway?

What differentiates selfishness from "normal" behavior?

Share a Bible verse on selfishness that speaks to you.

Part 1: Lesson 50
Self-Worth

Lamentations 3:21-26

"This I recall to my mind, therefore have I hope. It is of the LORD'S mercies that we are not consumed, because His compassions fail not." *They are new every morning: great is Thy faithfulness. The LORD is my portion, saith my soul; therefore will I hope in Him. The LORD is good unto them that wait for Him, to the soul that seeketh Him. It is good that a man should both hope and quietly wait for the salvation of the LORD."*

Many struggle with feelings of inferiority, personal weakness, unworthiness. Our faults and past mistakes loom over us, casting a shadow across our entire being. We simply cannot feel good about ourselves. Nothing seems to relieve us of this dead-weight of poor self-image. We drag it around with us like a ball-and-chain. Everything we do, say and think is somehow connected to this ball-and-chain. We are prisoners of our own self-image. But, In John 8:36, Jesus says: *"If the Son therefore shall make you, ye shall be freed indeed."*

He came to free you from your life-long ball-and-chain.

How do you define self-worth?

What is your own personal self-worth based on?
Are you glad you are you? Why or why not?

Do you feel you have a healthy sense of self-worth? Explain:

What scripture speaks to you and your interpretation of self-worth?

Part 1: Lesson 51
Serenity

1 Corinthians 14:33 KJV
"For God is not the author of confusion, but of peace."

Psalm 34:14
"Seek peace, and pursue it."

John 14:27
"Peace I leave with you, My peace I give unto you: not as the world giveth, give I unto you. Let not your heart be troubled, neither let it be afraid."

Philippians 4:4-7
"Rejoice in the LORD alway: and again I say, Rejoice. Let your moderation be known unto all men. The LORD is at hand. Be careful for nothing; but in everything by prayer and supplication with thanksgiving let your requests be made known unto God. And the peace of God, which passeth all understanding, shall keep your hearts and minds through Christ Jesus."

List the things that destroy your Serenity. Please be as thorough as possible:

What effect does this have on you and your Recovery?

What are your keys to Serenity for you in your Recovery?

What can you learn from the above scriptures about Peace and Serenity?

Can you apply it to your life when you are upset with certain people, places or things?

Part 1: Lesson 52
Spiritual Warfare

Ephesians 6:10-12 KJV

"Finally, my brethren, be strong in the Lord, and in the power of his might. Put on the whole armor of God, that ye may be able to stand against the wiles of the devil. For we wrestle not against flesh and blood, but against principalities, against powers, against the rulers of the darkness of this world, against spiritual wickedness in high places."

When we talk about spiritual warfare, we are not talking about swords and shields, tanks and guns. Nor are we talking about physical strength, endurance or prowess. We are talking about a river of strength from the Lord. He is our Shield and our spear, our tank and our guns.

Do you think spiritual warfare is real? Explain:

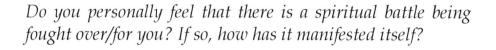

Do you personally feel that there is a spiritual battle being fought over/for you? If so, how has it manifested itself?

What does spiritual warfare have to do with your various recovery issues?

What tools or weapons do you use to fight this battle?

What have you learned about Spiritual Warfare today?

Note: for detailed Biblical studies of the 12 Steps see the Christians in Recovery 12 Steps Bible Studies

Book:
https://christians-in-recovery.org/12StepStudies

CD:
http://self-helpsoftware.com/12StepBibleStudies

Part 2: Working the Steps

Part 2: Lesson 1
Working the Steps

Romans 7:18-21 Weymouth

"For I know that in me, that is, in my lower self, nothing good has its home; for while the will to do right is present with me, the power to carry it out is not. For what I do is not the good thing that I desire to do; but the evil thing that I desire not to do, is what I constantly do. But if I do that which I desire not to do, it can no longer be said that it is I who do it, but the sin which has its home within me does it. I find therefore the law of my nature to be that when I desire to do what is right, evil is lying in ambush for me."

Step One:
We admitted we were powerless over our addictions and dysfunctions and that our lives had become unmanageable.

Recovery begins by admitting our own powerlessness. Coming face to face with our inability to control our lives which have reeled out of control and caused excruciating pain for ourselves as well as others.

*Have you **really** admitted powerlessness over your addictions / dysfunctions? Is pride standing in the way?*

Does starting recovery (or starting again) seem insurmountable or impossible? If so, why?

Does past failure portend future failure? Or can you be like a rubber ball that once it hits the cement floor, bounces even higher than the level from which it dropped?

Now read the rest of Paul's passage:

Romans 7:25-8:6 Weymouth

"Thanks be to God through Jesus Christ our Lord! To sum up then, with my understanding, I--my true self--am in servitude to the Law of God, but with my lower nature I am in servitude to the Law of sin. There is therefore now no condemnation to those who are in Christ Jesus; for the Spirit's Law--telling of Life in Christ Jesus--has set me free from the Law that deals only with sin and death. For what was impossible to the Law--powerless as it was because it acted through frail humanity--God effected. Sending His own Son in a body like that of sinful human nature and as a sacrifice for sin, He pronounced

sentence upon sin in human nature; in order that in our case the requirements of the Law might be fully met. For our lives are regulated not by our earthly, but by our spiritual natures. For if men are controlled by their earthly natures, they give their minds to earthly things. If they are controlled by their spiritual natures, they give their minds to spiritual things. Because for the mind to be given up to earthly things means death; but for it to be given up to spiritual things means Life and peace.

What had Paul learned?

How had he been set free from his sinful self?

As a Christian, does this apply to you as well?

For a comprehensive Twelve Step Study see:
http://Self-helpSoftware.com/12StepBibleStudies

Part 2: Lesson 2
Working the Steps

Step 3

"Made a decision to turn our will and our lives over to the care of God as we understood Him."

Many who have had a less than satisfactory relationship with their own father question Step 3. "Give up control to someone I can't see? To someone who would be like my own father who was never really there when I needed him? No way!"

Does turning your will and your life over to someone other than yourself seem intimidating to you? Why?

In Step 3 you are asked only to make the DECISION to do this. Does this make a difference?

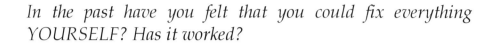

In the past have you felt that you could fix everything YOURSELF? Has it worked?

Are you willing to try another route?

Step 3 talks about turning yourself over to the CARE of God. Could this imply that God is loving in nature and is not like an abusive parent of the past?

Part 2: Lesson 3
Working the Steps

James 5:16 KJV

"Confess your faults one to another, and pray one for another, that ye may be healed. The effectual fervent prayer of a righteous man availeth much."

1 John 1:9 KJV

"If we confess our sins, he is faithful and just to forgive us our sins, and to cleanse us from all unrighteousness."

Step 5:

"We admitted to God, to ourselves, and to another human being the exact nature of our wrongs."

*In light of the above scriptures, why is it important to admit the **exact** nature of your wrongs?*

Why do you think you must admit these things to God, to yourself and to another person?

Relate an experience in your own recovery where you have taken Step 5 and what you learned from it.

Part 2: Lesson 4
Working the Steps

Step 11

"We sought through prayer and meditation to improve our conscious contact with God as we understood him, praying only for knowledge of his will for us and the power to carry that out."

Does Step 11 help you to have better relationships with others?

How does prayer help you to know God's will for you?

How does meditation improve your conscious contact with God? If so, how?

Has prayer and meditation help you to see the good things about yourself?

Write about a specific time when God actually showed you the correct path to follow.

Part 2: Lesson 5
Finding Strength in Each Day

Isaiah 40:29-31

"He giveth power to the faint; and to them that have no might He increaseth strength. Even the youths shall faint and be weary, and the young men shall utterly fall: But they that wait upon the LORD shall renew their strength; they shall mount up with wings as eagles; they shall run, and not be weary; and they shall walk, and not faint."

At times, especially early in recovery, it can be a challenge to find the strength and courage to face each new day in recovery.

Do you find it difficult to find strength each day? Why or why not?

What do you do to get energized or prepared for the day ahead of you?

What is your source of strength and how do you tap into it?

Part 2: Lesson 6
Struggling in Recovery

1 Peter 5:8-10 KJV

"Be sober, be vigilant; because your adversary the devil, as a roaring lion, walketh about, seeking whom he may devour: Whom resist stedfast in the faith, knowing that the same afflictions are accomplished in your brethren that are in the world. But the God of all grace, who hath called us unto His eternal glory by Christ Jesus, after that ye have suffered a while, make you perfect, establish, strengthen, settle you."

Recovery can be a real battle. For some it is painfully hard work from the start. For others the struggle and trials come after the pink cloud dissipates. And yet for others it is "easy" to overcome addiction and dysfunction. Complete one of the following sentences which is applicable to you and your recovery. Go into as much detail as you like:

I struggle because.......

I used to struggle but I no longer struggle because.....

Part 2: Lesson 7
Surrender

1 Samuel 12:24 KJV
"Only fear the LORD, and serve Him in truth with all your heart: for consider how great things He hath done for you."

One of the main themes in recovery is Surrender (the 3rd Step). In surrendering or turning our will and life over to the care of God we finally become victorious over our addictions and dysfunctions.

What does "surrender" mean to you as an individual who is in recovery (or trying to recover)?

Is it a one-time event or a process for you? Explain.

*Do you think it is realistic or possible to **completely** surrender?*

For you, is Acceptance the same as Surrender?

If you have a favorite scripture that helps you with surrender write it down here.

Part 2: Lesson 8
Taking Myself to God in Prayer

Jeremiah 33:3
"Call unto me, and I will answer thee, and shew thee great and mighty things, which thou knowest not."

Praying for others is easy, all it costs is a few moments of your time and then you get to give yourself brownie points for it. But if you are taking yourself to God in prayer that's risky. You might have your eyes opened to your own character defects. You might have to admit you were wrong about something or someone. If you take yourself to God in prayer you might have to **S-H-U-D-D-E-R** with the likelihood of **C-H-A-N-G-E!** You might have to make yourself vulnerable and humble.

Do you find it more difficult to pray for yourself and your own needs than to pray for others? Why or why not?

Do you feel intimidated when you come before the Lord? Are you afraid of what He might do in your life?

Are you leery of change--even though it is for the better?

Is humility a stumbling block for you?

Part 2: Lesson 9
Taking Time for Recovery

Luke 11:9-10 KJV

"Ask, and it shall be given you; seek, and ye shall find; knock, and it shall be opened unto you. For every one that asketh receiveth; and he that seeketh findeth; and to him that knocketh it shall be opened."

Life is busy. We never seem to have enough time for ourselves and our recovery can suffer.

*Do you take **enough** time for your own recovery?*

How much time do you invest in it each day?

What do you proactively do in order to nurture your recovery?

How can you improve the quality of the time and effort you put into it?

Can you afford not to take the time?

Part 2: Lesson 10
Temptation vs. Old Habits

James 1:12-16 Weymouth

"Blessed is he who patiently endures trials; for when he has stood the test, he will gain the victor's crown--even the crown of Life--which the Lord has promised to those who love Him. Let no one say when passing through trial, "My temptation is from God;" for God is incapable of being tempted to do evil, and He Himself tempts no one. But when a man is tempted, it is his own passions that carry him away and serve as a bait. Then the passion conceives, and becomes the parent of sin; and sin, when fully matured, gives birth to death. Do not be deceived, my dearly-loved brethren. Every gift which is good, and every perfect boon, is from above, and comes down from the Father, who is the source of all Light. In Him there is no variation nor the slightest suggestion of change."

1 Corinthians 10:13 KJV

"There hath no temptation taken you but such as is common to man: but God is faithful, who willnot suffer you to be tempted above that ye are able; but will with the temptation also make a way to escape, that ye may be able to bear it."

Can God tempt you?

Are you the only one who must face temptation?

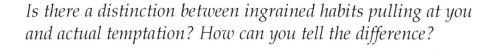

Is there a distinction between ingrained habits pulling at you and actual temptation? How can you tell the difference?

How can each one be defeated?

If recovery is WORK, if you are really sweating bullets, white knuckling it, do you think it is a sign that you have not turned your will and your life over to the care of God? Not letting the Holy Spirit take charge?

Part 2: Lesson 10
Triggers

Matthew 4:8

"Again, the devil took Him to a very high mountain and showed Him all the kingdoms of the world and their glory. And he said to Him, 'All these things I will give to You, if You will fall down and worship me.'

"Then Jesus said to him, 'Be gone, Satan! For it is written, "You shall worship the Lord your God and Him only shall you serve."'

Since a trigger is described as a successful temptation, we can use the powerful analogy from above. Even Jesus Christ was tempted. When temptation comes calling, as it surely will, we must respond as Jesus did. We must command them to be gone!

What triggers your addiction and/or dysfunctional behaviors? List them here.

Is it possible to anticipate these triggers ahead of time?

List ways in which you can defuse or eliminate these Individual triggers.

Write down favorite scripture that you use in times of great temptation.

Part 2: Lesson 11
The Truth

1 John 4:4 KJV
"Greater is He that is in you, than he that is in the world."

The more I work the 12 Steps and listen to God I realize was responsible for all the problems in my life, that my addiction/dysfunction had been a way of life for me for years, that I was dishonest in ways I never imagined, that my morals consisted of doing whatever I wanted just as long as I did not get caught.

Does this statement ring true for you?

How long have you been in an addictive or dysfunctional pattern of living? Write about it here:

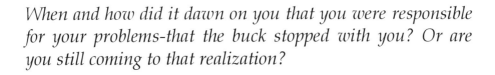

When and how did it dawn on you that you were responsible for your problems-that the buck stopped with you? Or are you still coming to that realization?

What role has dishonesty played in your addictive / dysfunctional behavior?

Was it "OK" as long as you did not get caught?

What convicted you of your error?

What was your turning point for change?

Part 2: Lesson 12
Spiritual Weapons

2 Corinthians 10:4-5 Weymouth

"The weapons with which we fight are not human weapons, but are mighty for God in overthrowing strong fortresses. For we overthrow arrogant 'reckonings,' and every stronghold that towers high in defiance of the knowledge of God, and we carry off every thought as if into slavery – into subjection to Christ..."

If you live in the Word of God, there is noting that can stand against you. Your greatest threat, your fortresses of insecurity, doubt and fear, will crumble beneath these non-human weapons of faith.

How does this scripture speak to you and your recovery?

What are the divine weapons that Paul is talking about?

What divine weapons are you using in your own personal struggles? Are you using them to the fullest?

Are there other weapons you could employ to keep you on track spiritually?

Part 2: Lesson 13
Which Way Home?

John 14:2-4 Weymouth

"In my Father's house there are many resting-places. Were it otherwise, I would have told you; for I am going to make ready a place for you. And if I go and make ready a place for you, I will return and take you to be with me, that where I am you also may be. And where I am going, you all know the way."

As Christians we are promised an eternal home with our Father in heaven. But I have to ask myself every so often which route am I taking home? Am I taking the short route? The easy route? The right route?

Which route are you taking?

Why are you taking this particular way Home?

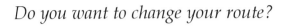

Do you want to change your route?

If so, how do you plan on doing it? (Make a plan below) A-B-C, 1-2-3:

Part 2: Lesson 14
Human Wisdom vs. Divine Wisdom

1 Corinthians 1:27-30 Weymouth

"But God has chosen the things which the world regards as foolish, in order to put its wise men to shame; and God has chosen the things which the world regards as destitute of influence, in order to put its powerful things to shame; and the things which the world regards as base, and those which it sets utterly at nought--things that have no existence--God has chosen in order to reduce to nothing things that do exist; to prevent any mortal man from boasting in the presence of God. But you--and it is all God's doing – are in Christ Jesus: He has become for us a wisdom which is from God, consisting of righteousness and sanctification and deliverance."

By understanding the will of God, verses that of our own, we can better diminish selfish wants and desires, releasing ego and pride, which makes room for the will of the Heavenly Father.

In your life, has God chosen what the world considers nonsense, weak, looks down on and despises? Explain and give specific examples:

Has Christ become your wisdom? If so, how?

Have you been put right with God or are you "still working on it?"

Part 3
Appraisal Worksheets

Look at the word-lists below. **Put a date by the things you are experiencing** on this particular day. Come back to this list every two weeks and go over it again to put a new date. You will see changes and growth taking shape.

You may copy these forms as needed for repeated use.

I Feel I am Struggling With:

Appraisal of:	Date									
obsessive traits										
addictions										
dysfunction										
addictive process										
unmanageability										
dysfunctional living										
excess										
false gods										
compulsive behavior										
control issues										
dishonesty										
revenge										
rationalization										
consequences										
powerlessness										
lies										
deception										
procrastination										
greed										
suffering										
bondage										
abuse										

arrogance										
idolatry										
character defects										
codependency										
slavery										
temptation burden										
discouragement										
backsliding										
insecurity										
helplessness										
fear										
loneliness										
hitting bottom										
hypocrisy										
relapse										
gluttony										
being a victim										
compulsion										
inadequacy										
self-deception										
self-destruction										
self-hatred										
shame										
dependencies										
addictive behavior										
bitterness										
doubt										
choices										
spiritual laziness										
anger										
denial										
oppression										
hopelessness										
selfishness										
sorrow										

List Other Character Defects/Weaknesses here:									

This Week I have Moved Closer to:

Appraisal of:	Date								
deliverance									
freedom									
hope									
healing									
perseverance									
humility									
wholeness									
inventory									
submission									
celebration									
reconciliation									
rest									
self-control									
boundaries									
honesty									
God's Word									
endurance									
accountability									
happiness									
contentment									
gratitude									
diligence									
self-esteem									
joy									

peace									
self-sufficiency									
redemption									
serenity									
self-protection									
transformation									
unity									
loyalty									
praise									
truth									
responsibility									
discipline									
service									
ability to enjoy									
repentance									
inheritance									
obedience									
comfort									
commitment									
salvation									
restitution									
self-preservation									
trust									
victory									
God's sufficiency									
guidance									
God's Power									
God's salvation									
Holy Spirit									
mentors									
direction									
God's Will									
God's friendship									
sponsors									
grace									
faithfulness									

List More Here:									

Definitions & Applications

1) Define each word below.
2) Explain what it means to you as a person in recovery and as a Christian.
3) How does it apply to you today? Is it something you need to address today?
4) Include a Scripture that you feel helps to express your thoughts.

Pride / Arrogance

Idolatry

Repentance

Obedience

Forgiveness

Grace

Mercy

Trust

Restoration

Thankfulness

Peace

Write down what you have learned about yourself and God result of doing this exercise:

How are you going to change?

What are you going to change? How are you going to do it (be specific)?

Daily Checklist

Carefully read Scripture and meditate on how it applies to my:

* Life
* Current Circumstances
* Recovery
* Feelings

Bible Studies for Recovery:
http://christians-in-recovery.org/BibleStudies

Recovery Devotionals:
http://recoverybooks.com/daily.html

Bibles for Recovery:
http://recoverybooks.com/bibles.html

*Spent time in prayer, quiet time with God (listening to Him)

*Made entries into my journal

See:
http://christians-in-recovery.org/Tools_Journal

*Worked one of the 12 Steps
See:
http://christians-in-recovery.org/Tools_12Steps_Info

*Attended a meeting either face to face or online CIR chat

Schedule:
http://christians-in-recovery.org/Members_Chat_Schedule

*Taken an inventory of my stress levels and stressors

Worksheets Available:
http://christians-in-recovery.org/Tools_Worksheets

*Checked in with my accountability partner/sponsor and spoken to them about

* The Step I am working on

* How I am *really* doing (temptations, stressors)

* What I am unhappy about

* What my shortfalls are

* What I can do to change

See:
http://christians-in-recovery.org/Tools_Sponsors_HelpfulStuff

* Talked with my family about what is going on in my life

* Honestly shared with my CIR friends and family

* What CIR meetings did I participate in today?

* Did I read and post to the CIR Message Boards?

* Did I talk privately with a fellow believer in recovery?

* Did I read my Bible and pray today?

*Done something to strengthen myself against future temptations? (e.g., thought about the true sources of my temptation, what I can do to eliminate it from my day and life, how I can avoid temptation in the future, etc.)

See:
http://christians-in-recovery.org/Issues_Temptation_KeysToOvercomingTemptation

Benefits & Responsibilities

My benefits of being in recovery:

My responsibilities because I am in Recovery:

Daily Truths Journal

Psalm 139: 1
"O Lord, thou hast searched me and known me."

When what we are saying is true, but not honest, we are lying.

Today's Date:

Scripture Read:

Other Materials Read:

Truths Found:

How will I allow this information to change my life?

Being Honest about My Addiction

Satan's sweet whispers of lies enter our minds, and if we do not deal with them properly, throwing them out, they become planted. Each time we return to that thought, to water it, it grows. It continues to grow until it blossoms into a plan. A plan, justified, then is put into action. The action becomes a pleasurable event which is repeated over and over to achieve that desired high. Each time a little more is required thus strengthening the rope that binds its victim, you.

What "Bad Seeds" did I allow to grow in my head today?

I gave in to this temptation and allowed it to become sin. Please explain how this sin affected you Spiritually:

Take time right now to ask God's forgiveness. Thank God for His Grace to you!

Psalms 51:17
"The sacrifices of God are a broken spirit: a broken and contrite heart, O God, thou wilt not despise."

Make a plan to better equip yourself the next time this temptation crosses in front of you or crosses your mind.

1) Tell yourself NO! Out loud if needed.

2) Ask God for a scripture to fit this temptation.

3) Avoid this person, place or thing as if it will kill you. It will kill you, either physically, mentally or spiritually if you continue to allow it in your life.

John 8:32
"You will know the truth, and the truth will set you free."

Victories Won Today!
"I am weak but thou are strong."

With God's strength, I won these victories over temptations:

What I used to overcome this temptation:

Scripture used:

Thoughts used:

Action Taken:

I will call this plan to use in the future:

Additional copies of this book may be ordered online:

http://christians-in-recovery.org/Workbook

To order the workbook as software for use
on your computer go online:

http://Self-helpSoftware.com/Workbook

Thank God for His strength and mercy!

Thank Him for making a way of escape!

You may also benefit from the:

Christians in Recovery
Devotional Journal

365 Recovery Thoughts, Scriptures & Prayers to Change Your Life

Order Online: http://christians-in-recovery.org/Devotional

This devotional journal is for those who are seeking healing and wholeness in their life as well as a closer relationship with God.

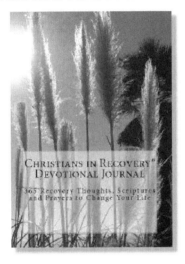

Are you addicted to a substance or behavior?

Are you a victim of anxiety, fear or hopelessness?

Is a behavior or thought pattern controlling your life?

Are you codependent or an adult child?

Do you over eat?

Strengthen your faith as you draw nearer to God through the pages of this book. Three hundred and sixty five individual recovery thoughts with accompanying scriptures and prayers to guide you.

Each day has a section for you to include your own thoughts, notes, prayers and favorite scriptures. Includes Topical Index as well as Scripture Index. 6" X 9", 384 pages.

Made in the USA
Columbia, SC
14 July 2018